Travel Guide To Menorca

GW00497777

All Rights Reserved . No part Of This Publication Can Be Reproduced, Transmitted or Distributed Without Prior Written Permission Of The Publisher , Except Incase of Brief Review, Quotation And Certain Other Non Commercial Uses By Copyright Law.

Table Of Contents

Introduction

Menorca is a hidden gem in the Spanish Balearic Islands, located in the heart of the Mediterranean Sea. This breathtaking island is known for its stunning beaches, crystal-clear waters, and beautiful natural landscapes, making it the perfect destination for travelers seeking a peaceful and authentic Mediterranean experience.

The island is a true paradise for beach lovers, with over 200 beaches and coves dotted along its coastline. From secluded bays to bustling stretches of sand, Menorca's beaches are some of the most beautiful in the world. The turquoise waters are perfect for swimming, snorkeling, and diving, and the soft white sand beaches are ideal for sunbathing and relaxing.

But Menorca is more than just a beach destination. The island is also rich in history and boasts a number of prehistoric monuments, including the famous Naveta d'Es Tudons and Torre d'en Galmés. These ancient structures offer a glimpse into the island's past and are a testament to its rich cultural heritage. Visitors can explore these fascinating sites and learn more about the island's history and culture.

Menorca's charming towns and villages are also a highlight of the island. With their narrow streets, historic architecture, and lively markets, these towns offer a glimpse into traditional Spanish life. Visitors can wander through the picturesque streets, admiring the colorful buildings and soaking up the vibrant atmosphere. The island's cuisine is also a highlight, with fresh seafood, local cheeses, and traditional dishes such as caldereta de langosta (lobster stew) and mahón cheese.

Outdoor enthusiasts will find plenty of activities to enjoy in Menorca, from hiking and cycling to water sports and boat trips. The island's diverse landscapes, including rocky cliffs, pine forests, and sandy coves, provide the perfect setting for exploring and adventure. Visitors can hike along the Camí de Cavalls, a historic trail that circles the island, or explore the island's stunning coastline by boat. The island's waters are also perfect for kayaking, paddleboarding, and snorkeling, and there are plenty of companies offering equipment rental and guided tours.

For those seeking a more relaxed experience, Menorca's spas and wellness centers offer the perfect opportunity to unwind and recharge. Visitors can indulge in a range of treatments and therapies, including massages, facials, and yoga classes, all set against the backdrop of Menorca's stunning natural beauty.

Menorca is also a popular destination for families, with plenty of activities and attractions to keep children entertained. The island's water parks, zoos, and adventure parks are a hit with kids of all ages, and there are also plenty of family-friendly beaches and restaurants.

Why Visit Menorca?

One of the main reasons to visit Menorca is its breathtaking beaches, which are renowned for their crystal-clear turquoise waters and powdery white sands. From popular spots like Cala Macarella and Cala Mitjana to hidden gems like Cala Pregonda and Cala Turqueta, there is a beach for every preference, offering tranquility and natural beauty. Visitors can spend their days lounging on the beach, swimming, snorkeling, or kayaking in the hidden coves and bays.

Menorca was designated a UNESCO Biosphere Reserve in 1993, recognizing its outstanding natural and cultural value. The island is home to diverse ecosystems, including wetlands, dunes, and forests, making it a paradise for nature enthusiasts. Explore the S'Albufera des Grau Nature Reserve or hike along the Cami de Cavalls coastal path to appreciate Menorca's pristine environment. Visitors can spot over 220 species of birds, including booted eagles, red kites, and Egyptian vultures, and over 1,000 varieties of plants.

Immerse yourself in Menorca's ancient past by visiting its impressive talayotic ruins. These prehistoric monuments, including the iconic Naveta d'es Tudons and Torre d'en Galmés, offer a glimpse into the island's early civilization and serve as a testament to Menorca's rich history and cultural heritage. Visitors can also explore the island's charming historic towns and villages, such as Ciutadella and Mahón, to discover the local architecture, shops, and restaurants.

Experience the vibrant local culture by participating in Menorca's traditional festivals. The island comes alive with celebrations such as Sant Joan, a midsummer fiesta with bonfires and traditional horseback parades, and the Festes de Sant Antoni, where locals honor the patron saint with traditional dances and street processions. These festivities provide a unique insight into the island's customs and traditions.

Menorca's cuisine reflects its rich agricultural heritage and Mediterranean influences. Visitors can indulge in traditional dishes such as the famous lobster stew (Caldereta de Llagosta), Mahón cheese, and the local gin, Xoriguer. Explore the tapas bars and seafood restaurants to savor the flavors of Menorca while enjoying stunning sea views.

From hiking and biking to water sports and horseback riding, Menorca offers a wide range of outdoor activities to suit every adventurer. Explore the stunning coastline through kayaking or snorkeling in hidden coves, or venture inland to discover the island's rugged trails and natural parks.

Menorca remains relatively untouched by mass tourism, allowing visitors to experience an authentic island atmosphere. The laid-back lifestyle, friendly locals, and a slower pace of life make Menorca an ideal destination for those seeking relaxation and an escape from the hustle and bustle of everyday life.

History Of Menorca

Menorca's history is a compelling tapestry of traditions, architecture, and cultural practices that reflect the influence of various civilizations that have shaped the island over the centuries.

One of the most significant aspects of Menorca's history is its ancient talayotic culture, characterized by the construction of megalithic stone monuments and settlements. These talayotic structures, including taulas (T-shaped stone monuments) and talayots (stone towers), are abundant across the island, serving as enduring testimony to the island's earliest inhabitants. The talayotic period, which dates back to the Bronze and Iron Ages, is a defining feature of Menorca's identity, and it is a source of fascination for locals and visitors alike.

Visitors can explore many of these archaeological sites, such as Torre d'en Galmés and Naveta des Tudons, to learn about Menorca's ancient past. These sites provide insight into the island's prehistoric culture and way of life, with many of them featuring informative exhibits and displays that help visitors understand their significance. The Torre d'en Galmés is one of the most impressive talayotic sites on the island, featuring a multitude of talayots, as well as a T-shaped taula, which is believed to have been used for religious ceremonies. The Naveta des Tudons, on the other hand, is a unique burial chamber that dates back to around 1200 BC, and it is one of the best-preserved navetas on the island.

Another key aspect of Menorca's history is its colonial heritage. Menorca's strategic location in the Mediterranean made it an attractive prospect for various colonial powers throughout history, including the Phoenicians, Romans, Moors, and Byzantines. However, it was under the rule of the British during the 18th century that Menorca experienced a particularly influential period. The British occupation of Menorca lasted from 1708 to 1802, and it left a lasting legacy on the island's architecture, town planning, and cultural practices.

The influence of British rule can still be seen in the island's towns, particularly in the capital city of Mahón, where the legacy of British rule is evident in its Georgian-style buildings, stone walls, and military fortifications. Mahón is a charming town that is rich in history and heritage, and it boasts a plethora of fascinating museums and cultural attractions that are well worth exploring. One of the most notable landmarks in Mahón is the Sant Francesc Church, a beautiful Baroque-style church that dates back to the 18th century. The church features an impressive bell tower that offers stunning views of the city and the harbor.

Menorca's cultural calendar is marked by a vibrant array of traditional festivals and celebrations that pay homage to the island's heritage. One standout event is the Festes de Sant Joan, held annually in Ciutadella, the former capital of Menorca. The festival takes place on June 23rd and 24th and is characterized by its spirited horse parades and jaleo, a unique equestrian display where riders attempt to "cap" the horses with hooks. This celebration is a testament to Menorca's equestrian tradition, and it is cherished as a symbol of local identity and pride.

The island's folklore and music also play a significant role in preserving its cultural heritage, with traditional Menorcan music and dance forms, such as jota and ball de bot, continuing to be performed and celebrated at various cultural events and fiestas. One of the most popular folk dance groups on the island is Grup Folklòric Sant Joanet, which performs traditional Menorcan dances and songs at various events and festivals throughout the year.

Today, the preservation of Menorca's historical and cultural legacy is closely guarded, with initiatives aimed at safeguarding its talayotic sites, promoting local crafts and traditions, and honoring its distinct cultural identity. The Menorca Talayótica Foundation, for example, is a non-profit organization that is dedicated to the research, conservation, and dissemination of Menorca's talayotic heritage. The foundation works closely with local communities, institutions, and experts to ensure that Menorca's ancient past is preserved for future generations.

Getting There

Menorca, a breathtaking island located in the Balearic archipelago, is well-connected by air and sea, offering travelers numerous options to reach this captivating destination.

By Air:
Menorca Airport (Aeropuerto de Menorca, or Mahón Airport) is the primary airport serving the island, situated near the capital city of Mahón. The airport offers a wide range of domestic and international flights, with direct connections to various cities in Europe, including Barcelona, Madrid, London, Paris, and other major hubs. Several airlines, including British Airways, EasyJet, Monarch, and Ryanair, operate regular flights to Menorca, making it convenient to reach the island from different parts of the continent.

During the peak travel season, many charter and low-cost carriers offer affordable flight options to Menorca, providing budget-friendly travel opportunities for visitors. Travelers may also choose connecting flights through nearby airports in Spain, making it a hassle-free journey to reach this stunning island.

By Sea:
Menorca is also accessible by sea, with regular ferry services connecting the island to the nearby Spanish port cities of Barcelona, Valencia, and Palma de Mallorca, as well as other ports within the Balearic Islands. The ports of Mahón and Ciutadella serve as the island's main ferry terminals, accommodating both passenger and cargo vessels.

Ferry operators provide various types of services, including high-speed ferries, traditional car ferries, and catamarans, offering passengers a choice of comfortable and efficient sea travel to Menorca. The sea journey to the island offers a scenic approach, allowing travelers to enjoy stunning views of Menorca's coastline as they arrive at either of the island's port towns.

Transportation Options

Car and Scooter Hire

Without a doubt, the most comfortable form of transport is a car or scooter that can be hired directly from the airport on arrival or from your Menorca holiday villa resort. With your own set of wheels, you will be able to explore all corners of the island at your leisure with no waiting around for buses or taxis. Whether you are travelling as a family, a large group of friends, or as a couple, there are vehicles available to suit all! Prices for 5 door car hire start from 30€ per day, and for those more adventurous, a 125cc scooter during May and October is as low as 20€ per day. A tip for when you are searching for the best car hire on the island is to be sure to read the small print. Some of the larger multi-national companies claim to offer the best prices, however, on arrival you may be presented with extra charges with the added inconvenience of a long wait for a shuttle bus to the outskirts of the airport vicinity. Our recommendation is to go local! Local family-run car hire companies often offer the best rates and conditions with a brilliant service.

Buses

During the summer season, bus services are available from all beach resorts to the main municipalities. The plus side of public transport is that you can avoid the hassle of driving and parking in the town centres, however, the downside is that getting from A to B will take considerably longer than if you hire a vehicle or take a taxi. Although there are few bus connections between holiday resorts, more often than not, you will first have to travel to one of the island's larger towns and then connect with another bus towards the coast. The same scenario applies from the airport, first a bus to Mahón bus station and then another one or two buses to your Menorca holiday villa. The bus companies serving the island are TMSA (all municipality towns and south coast), Autos Fornells (north-east coast, Mahón, Alaior, and Es Mercadal), and Autocares Torres (Ciutadella, west coast, Mahón airport, and Mahón), and tariffs range from 1.30€ for shorter journeys to 5.40€ from Mahón to Ciutadella. Updated route timetables and tariffs are available on the company websites.

Taxis and Transfers

Taking a radio taxi or transfer from the airport to your Menorca holiday villa is very easy as both are available directly outside the arrivals terminal. Taxis are available on-demand, and transfers, which are the perfect option for large parties, must be reserved in advance. There are also premium transfer companies offering services in high range vehicles to and from Mahón airport.

When it comes to sightseeing and exploring, if you plan to move around the island quite a bit, the overall cost of doing so with a taxi or transfer could become pretty pricey as there is no UBER service on the island! Be sure to cost up your options first, as it is probably more cost-effective to hire a vehicle for the duration or part of your stay. There are taxi stands in the centre of all towns and resorts, look for the white cars with a green light on top, which is illuminated when the taxi is available.

Boat Rental: Explore Menorca from the Sea

An exciting and unique option to get around Menorca is to rent a boat. With its location in the middle of the Mediterranean Sea, the island offers the perfect opportunity to discover its coasts and coves from a different perspective.

Chartering a boat gives you the freedom to explore hidden coves, secluded beaches, and remote locations not easily accessible by land.Boat rental companies in Menorca In Menorca, you will find several boat rental companies that offer a wide range of boats. We recommend Donboats.

Boat rental allows you to create your own route and enjoy the natural beauty of the Menorcan coast at your own pace. You will be able to stop in coves with turquoise waters, practice snorkeling and marvel at the steep cliffs that border the island.Remember to plan your route in advance, bring enough fuel and respect the navigation regulations established in the area. Also, make sure you are aware of the weather conditions and tides before you set sail.Boat rental in Menorca offers an unforgettable experience and allows you to discover the island from a unique perspective. If you have the opportunity and the necessary skills to drive a boat, do not hesitate to consider this transport option to enjoy a day full of adventure and marine discoveries.

Bicycle Rental

Menorca is an ideal place to explore by bike. With its beautiful landscape and its pleasant climate, you will be able to enjoy bike rides while you discover the charms of the island.

Many local companies offer bicycle rental services, and there are many well-signposted routes that will take you to places of interest and secluded beaches.You have to know that there are 6 main routes to go from one end of the island to the other:

Es Castell – Sant Lluís (6 km)
Es Mercadal – Alaior (7,7 km)
Ciutadella – Ferreries (16,5 km)
Mahón – Es Castell (4 km)
Ferreries – Es Mercadal (15,5 km)
Alaior – Mahón (12 km)

Bicycle rental companies in Menorca

We recommend these companies for bike rental on the island. Enjoy the best routes with:

-Tot Velo
-Sports Kayak Menorca
-Velos Joan
-Stop and Go bikes

Getting Around

As you begin planning your trip to the stunning island of Menorca, it's important to consider the various transportation options available to you. With a range of choices including public transport, bike hire, car rental, taxis, transfer services and even boat rental, you're sure to find an option that suits your unique needs and preferences.

Each transportation option has its own distinct advantages and considerations to keep in mind. If you're interested in taking public transport, be sure to carefully review the timetables and plan your routes in advance to avoid any unexpected delays. For those who prefer a more scenic experience, bike hire is an excellent choice, but it's important to remember to bring a map and follow all road safety rules.

If you're looking for the ultimate in freedom and flexibility, car rental might be the perfect option for you. However, it's essential to compare prices and read the conditions carefully, and to always abide by the traffic regulations and parking limitations on the island. Alternatively, if you value convenience above all else, taxis and transfer services can be a great choice, especially if you're traveling with a group.

For those seeking a truly exclusive experience, boat rental is a unique option that allows you to explore the island from the sea. With so many transportation options at your disposal, you're sure to find the perfect way to get around Menorca and make the most of your time on this beautiful island.

No matter which option you choose, we highly recommend taking the time to explore Menorca at your own pace and discover all that this Mediterranean paradise has to offer. From the stunning beaches and coves with crystal-clear waters, to the charming towns, nature trails and rich cultural heritage, Menorca is a destination that truly has it all. So go ahead, enjoy your trip, and be sure to capture plenty of unforgettable moments along the way!

Accommodations

Menorca offers a variety of hotels catering to diverse preferences. From beachfront resorts with stunning views to charming boutique options in historic towns, Menorca's hotels provide a range of accommodations for a memorable stay.

1. Hotel Artiem Carlos III:

Situated on the waterfront in Es Castell, Menorca, the Hotel Artiem Carlos III offers guests a luxurious and tranquil stay. This adults-only hotel boasts stunning views of the sea, giving you a chance to enjoy the calming ocean breeze from the comfort of your room. The hotel has easy access to a small beach, allowing you to take a refreshing dip in the crystal-clear waters of the Mediterranean.

The hotel features a pool, a wellness center, and a rooftop terrace with a bar, providing the perfect place to unwind and enjoy a drink while taking in the breathtaking views. The rooms are modern and comfortable, with a minimalist touch that complements the serene atmosphere of the hotel. The hotel also offers a restaurant serving local and international cuisine, with dishes prepared using fresh, locally-sourced ingredients.

2. Insotel Punta Prima Resort:

If you're looking for a family-friendly resort with a range of amenities, Insotel Punta Prima Resort is an excellent option. Situated in Punta Prima, this resort features multiple swimming pools, a spa, fitness facilities, and entertainment for both adults and children. The spacious rooms and apartments are equipped with all the necessary comforts, making it easy for families to feel at home. There are several restaurants serving diverse cuisines, ensuring that everyone can find something to suit their tastes. With so many activities, amenities, and dining options, guests will never run out of things to do at this resort.

3. Royal Son Bou Family Club:

For families looking for a fun-filled vacation, Royal Son Bou Family Club is an ideal choice. Located near Son Bou Beach, this resort offers a wide range of activities and entertainment, including multiple swimming pools, sports facilities, a kids' club, and spacious apartments equipped with kitchenettes. The resort also has various dining options available on-site, catering to both adults and children. With so much to do at the resort and nearby, families are sure to have a memorable vacation.

4. Hotel Artiem Capri:

Located in the heart of Mahón, Hotel Artiem Capri is a boutique hotel offering a chic and tranquil environment for guests. The hotel's rooftop terrace features a pool and bar, providing panoramic views of the city and bay. The gym and wellness center are perfect for those looking to stay active and healthy during their stay. The hotel's restaurant serves healthy and locally-sourced cuisine, made with fresh, seasonal ingredients. The rooms are tastefully decorated and provide a peaceful retreat for guests looking to escape the hustle and bustle of daily life.

5. Barcelo Hamilton Menorca:

If you're looking for an adults-only hotel in Es Castell, Barcelo Hamilton Menorca is a fantastic choice. The hotel offers a relaxing atmosphere, with a spa, pool, and rooftop terrace providing picturesque views of the surrounding area. The contemporary, comfortable rooms are perfect for couples looking to unwind and enjoy some quality time together. The hotel's buffet restaurant and cocktail bar offer a range of delicious dining options, making it easy for guests to enjoy a romantic evening .

Villas and Rentals

Renting a villa can be an excellent choice. Villas in Menorca offer a level of comfort, privacy, and luxury that many travelers find appealing. They provide a home away from home, with all the modern amenities you need to enjoy your Menorcan adventure.

Villas in Menorca come in all shapes and sizes, from small and cozy to large and luxurious. They are typically well-equipped with modern amenities such as fully equipped kitchens, private swimming pools, and outdoor dining areas. Many villas also offer stunning views of the surrounding countryside or the sea, providing a peaceful and idyllic setting for your stay.

When it comes to renting a villa in Menorca, there are several options available. You can choose to rent directly from the property owner or through a rental agency. Rental agencies often have a wide selection of villas to choose from and can help you find the perfect property to suit your needs and budget. They can also provide additional services such as airport transfers, housekeeping, and concierge services to make your stay even more comfortable and convenient.

In terms of location, there are villas scattered throughout the island, from the bustling towns of Mahón and Ciutadella to the more secluded and peaceful areas of the countryside. Some of the most popular areas for villa rentals in Menorca include the beach resorts of Cala Galdana, Cala'n Bosch, and Son Bou, as well as the charming towns of Alaior and Es Mercadal. Each location offers a unique experience, allowing you to tailor your Menorcan adventure to your preferences and interests.

In terms of cost, villa rentals in Menorca can vary widely depending on the size of the property, its location, and the time of year. Generally, prices tend to be higher during the peak summer months, so booking your villa well in advance is recommended. However, with careful planning and research, you can find a villa that suits your budget and provides a memorable and comfortable stay.

Renting a villa in Menorca can be a fantastic way to experience the island in style and comfort. Whether you're traveling with family, friends, or as a couple, a villa rental can provide the perfect base for your Menorcan adventure. So, whether you're looking for a beachfront retreat or a secluded countryside escape, there are plenty of options to choose from when it comes to villa rentals in Menorca. Here are list of carefully selected villas to consider.

1. Villa Las Cumbres - This stunning villa is located in the heart of Menorca, near Es Mercadal. With its spacious interiors, modern amenities, and breathtaking views of the countryside and Monte Toro, this property offers the perfect combination of luxury and relaxation. The villa features five bedrooms, each with its own private bathroom, as well as a cozy living room, a fully-equipped kitchen, and a spacious dining area. Outside, guests can enjoy a large swimming pool surrounded by well-manicured gardens, as well as a barbecue area and a covered terrace with plenty of seating. With its central location, this villa is just a short drive away from Menorca's best beaches, restaurants, and attractions.

2. Villa Son Bou Beach - This beautiful villa is situated in the heart of Son Bou, one of Menorca's most popular beach resorts. With its proximity to the stunning sandy beach, as well as a range of nearby restaurants and shops, this property is perfect for those looking to enjoy both relaxation and convenience during their stay. The villa features three bedrooms, two bathrooms, a cozy living room, and a fully-equipped kitchen. Outside, guests can enjoy a large swimming pool surrounded by a spacious terrace with plenty of sun loungers and seating. With its prime location, this villa is the ideal base for exploring the island and enjoying all that Menorca has to offer.

3. Villa Alaior - This charming villa is located in the heart of Alaior, one of Menorca's most picturesque towns. With its blend of traditional Menorcan architecture and modern comfort, this property offers a unique and authentic experience. The villa features four bedrooms, each with its own private bathroom, as well as a cozy living room, a fully-equipped kitchen, and a spacious dining area. Outside, guests can enjoy a large swimming pool surrounded by a beautiful garden, as well as a covered terrace with plenty of seating. With its central location, this villa is just a short walk away from Alaior's historic center, as well as its shops, restaurants, and amenities.

4. Villa Cala Galdana - Nestled in the picturesque bay of Cala Galdana, this villa offers breathtaking sea views and direct access to the beach. The property features spacious interiors, a large terrace for al fresco dining, and easy access to the crystal-clear waters of the Mediterranean.

5. Villa Binibeca Vell - Set in the idyllic fishing village of Binibeca, this villa exudes charm and tranquility. With its whitewashed walls, traditional architecture, and proximity to the sea, this property offers a peaceful and authentic Menorcan experience.

6. Villa Es Grau - Ideal for those seeking a quiet and natural setting, this villa is located near the unspoiled beach and nature reserve of Es Grau. Surrounded by lush countryside and offering a private pool, this property allows for a peaceful retreat amidst Menorca's natural beauty.

7. Villa Ciutadella - For those wanting to explore the historic and vibrant town of Ciutadella, this villa offers a convenient and stylish base. With its modern amenities, garden, and proximity to the town's attractions, guests can enjoy both cultural immersion and relaxation.

These are just a few options among the many beautiful villas available for rent in Menorca, each offering a distinct experience to suit different preferences and travel styles.

Budget Options

If you're planning a trip to Menorca on a budget, there are several affordable accommodation options available that can help you save money without sacrificing comfort or convenience. Here are some of the most popular and budget-friendly options:

1. Hostels: Menorca is home to several hostels located in popular tourist areas like Ciutadella and Mahón. Hostels can be a great choice for budget-conscious travelers, as they offer dormitory-style accommodations as well as private rooms at reasonable rates. You can easily meet other travelers and enjoy a sociable atmosphere while staying in a hostel.

2. Guesthouses and Bed & Breakfasts: If you prefer a more personal touch, there are many guesthouses and B&Bs scattered across the island, particularly in smaller towns and rural areas. These accommodations often provide comfortable rooms and a warm, personal atmosphere at more affordable prices than larger hotels. You can expect to receive a friendly welcome and personalized recommendations for exploring the island.

3. Apartment Rentals: Renting a self-catered apartment can be a cost-effective option, especially for families or groups of friends. Many apartments in Menorca are well-equipped with kitchens, allowing guests to prepare their own meals and save on dining expenses. You can also enjoy more privacy and flexibility with an apartment rental.

4. Rural Accommodations: Menorca's rural countryside is home to numerous agrotourism properties and rural guesthouses. These accommodations often offer a peaceful environment, traditional charm, and the opportunity to experience the island's natural beauty at budget-friendly rates. You can disconnect from the hustle and bustle of urban life and enjoy a more relaxed pace of living.

5. Camping: For nature enthusiasts, Menorca offers a selection of campsites situated in scenic locations near the coast or amidst the island's countryside. Camping is an affordable option for those seeking to immerse themselves in Menorca's outdoor beauty and enjoy a more back-to-nature experience. You can wake up to the sounds of birds chirping and stunning views of the Mediterranean sea.

Hostels in Menorca:
1. Hostal La Isla - located in the heart of Ciutadella, this hostel offers budget-friendly accommodation with a communal kitchen and free Wi-Fi.
2. Hostal Jume - situated in the historic center of Mahón, this charming hostel features comfortable rooms and a rooftop terrace with views of the city.
3. Hostal Llucmacanes Gran - nestled in the countryside near Es Castell, this cozy hostel offers a peaceful retreat with a garden and outdoor pool.

Guest Houses in Menorca:
1. Casa Albertí - located in the old town of Ciutadella, this guest house offers elegant rooms with traditional Menorcan décor and a courtyard garden.
2. Hostal La Lluna - set in a historic building in Mahón, this guest house features stylish rooms with modern amenities and a terrace overlooking the city.
3. Casa Ses 3 Voltes - situated in the charming village of Alaior, this guest house offers comfortable accommodation with a communal kitchen and a sun terrace.

Apartment Rentals in Menorca:
1. Apartamentos Royal Maui - located in the popular resort of Cala'n Bosch, these modern apartments offer a pool and easy access to the beach.
2. Apartamentos Son Bou Gardens - situated in the resort of Son Bou, these spacious apartments feature a garden, pool, and are close to the beach.
3. Aptos. La Noria - nestled in the heart of Cala Galdana, these apartments offer a peaceful setting with a pool and are within walking distance to the beach.

Rural Accommodation in Menorca:
1. Agroturismo Biniatram - located in the countryside near Es Mercadal, this rural accommodation offers charming rooms in a traditional Menorcan farmhouse.
2. Finca Atalis - set in a rural setting near Sant Lluis, this rural accommodation features rustic rooms and a pool surrounded by gardens.
3. Agroturismo Ca Na Xini - nestled in the countryside near Ferreries, this rural accommodation offers comfortable rooms and a peaceful atmosphere.

Camping Options in Menorca:
1. Camping Son Bou - located near the popular beach of Son Bou, this campsite offers pitches for tents and caravans, as well as bungalows for rent.
2. Camping Sa Pedrera - situated in a natural setting near Es Mercadal, this campsite offers spacious pitches and is within walking distance to the beach.
3. Camping Cala Blanca - set in a pine forest near the beach of Cala Blanca, this campsite offers facilities for tents and caravans, as well as access to the nearby town's amenities.

Exploring Menorca

Must-see Beaches

Menorca is a small island in the Balearic archipelago that boasts over 100 coves, or "calas" as they are known in Spanish. With such a vast number of calas to choose from, it's impossible to say which one is the best. Each one has its own unique charm and beauty, making Menorca a true paradise for beach lovers.

One way to categorize the calas is by dividing them into southern and northern calas. This division is based on the island's geography, which is short and wide, like a giant croissant. The southern calas are closer to the main urban areas, while the northern calas are more secluded and remote. Depending on your preferences, you can choose between the bustling atmosphere of the southern calas or the tranquil seclusion of the northern ones.

Regardless of which cala you choose, you'll be greeted by crystal-clear waters that range from deep blue to vibrant turquoise. The water is so clear that you can see the seabed, and the marine life that inhabits it. Snorkeling is a popular activity in Menorca, and all the calas are worth exploring. You'll find an array of fish in the different calas, from colorful tropical species to schools of silver sardines.

The south of Menorca is home to some stunning calas with turquoise waters and green trees. Most of these beaches are easily accessible by car and require a walk of less than 30 minutes to reach. However, some of them may only be accessible on foot or have limited street parking, so it's best to check before heading out.

In my opinion, the best beaches in the south of Menorca are:

1. Cala Mitjana and Cala Mitjaneta: These two calas are famous for their beautiful surroundings and calm waters. It takes around 15 minutes to walk to them from the starting point of Camí de Cavalls, and they are perfect for spending an entire day.They are probably two of the very best calas in Menorca! The waters are calm because the calas are protected by the rocks and there are spots to jump into the water, epic views and overall, it is a great place to spend an entire day.

Cala Macarella and Cala Macarelleta
These are the other brothers of the island, and considered also some of the best beaches in the Mediterranean. Like the two previous calas, Macarella and Macarelleta are two calas next to each other, with blue waters surrounded by trees. The scenary of cala Macarelleta is just awesome.my honest tip for those who are not early birds... avoid the small one and go to Macarella. We went there at 9:30 am by boat and Macarelleta was already packed, on a Friday! I can't imagine how busy it can be at noon on the weekend. To get to them, there a different options: by boat, by bus and walking, or from the Cami de Cavalls (35 mins).

Cala Fustam

This tiny cala is only 25 meters wide and hard to get to. You won't find so many people here because the views from the sand are not as epic as the other calas. Then, why is Cala Fustam in this ranking of best calas in Mallorca? Because if you come here by boat, the scenery is unique. Pristine waters, a little sandy beach surrounded by trees and tranquility. If you want a moment to relax, eat, listen to your music and feel free from the crowds, this is your place!

If you prefer a bigger cala and you don't mind walking 1 hour – from Cala Mitjana parking – Cala Escorxada is fascinating. The sand is white and the water is crystalline. We saw tons of fish in this cala and it well deserves a mention here, even more if you come by boat. The access by foot is one of the longest of the island to get to a beach, but that also means privacy.

Cala En Turqueta

Cala Turqueta is many people's best cala in Menorca, for good reasons. The name Turqueta comes from its turquoise water that contrasts with the clear sand. The cala has pines that offer shade and has its own parking. You'll need just 10 minutes to come to this paradise... if you find a parking place. Same as Cala Macarelleta, come early. Otherwise, you won't find a spot.

Cala Blanca

Cala blanca, next to Ciutadella, is maybe the less epic cala on this list, but deserves to be mentioned as one of the best calas and beaches in Menorca. We suggest avoiding the beach – appears as Platja Blanca – and instead, go to a private spot along the rock walls like the one we found. To reach this secret place, you have to pass the Dive Center Cala Blanca and go downstairs.

Es Caló Blanc

Moving to the East, there are two calas , one is Es Caló Blanc, due to the quality the water – epic crystal clear – and being the smallest beach of Menorca. This small beach is only **5 meters wide!** Because of this, people lay on the rocks around it. It's easy to access thanks to its nearby parking, in Saint Lluis.

Cala de La Olla – Sa Olla

The other option in the eastern part of the island, and next to Es Caló Blanc, is Cala de La Olla. This great place for snorkelling is not well known to tourists and its easy to get to. Again, there is a parking area very close to the cala. We suggest walking for some meters, avoiding the people who stay at the first stairs. You'll be able to sit on a better place and have your own personal piece of pool

While the south of the island boasts numerous calas and beaches with clear sand and pines, the north offers a completely different, yet equally mesmerizing landscape. The beaches in this area combine red and brown colors with transparent waters, creating a unique and striking view. The northern calas are less crowded than the southern ones due to the need to drive and walk more to reach them, which makes them perfect for those seeking solitude.

If you're planning to explore the northern beaches of Menorca, you might want to check out our list of the best beaches in that area. One of the most amazing beaches in the north is Cala Pilar. This virgin beach has red sand and incredible waters, but reaching it takes a 45-minute walk from the parking. During the high season, the parking is managed by a person who controls the access and allows or denies cars from entering. There is no shade or drinkable water on this beach, so it's essential to bring enough sunscreen and water.

Another noteworthy beach is Cala Pregonda, which is considered the top beach in the north of Menorca. This beach is simply breathtaking, and seeing the photo below will convince you. To reach Cala Pregonda, you need to park in the Platja Benimel·la parking and then walk for about 30 intense minutes. It's better to avoid walking between 12-2 pm because of the scorching sun. You'll definitely need lots of water during the hike.

Cala Pregonda is like nothing you've ever seen before. It feels like being on Mars, with decorative rocks in the middle, sand for the sand lovers, and rocks for those who love to explore. It's an excellent place for snorkeling, and you'll be amazed by the underwater life.

Finally, there's Platja de Cavalleria, which is the starting point of a series of calas that are next to each other, forming a fascinating route. To reach these calas, you need to walk from one to another, and there are two main beaches: Platja de Benimel·la and Platja de Cavalleria, both with their own parkings. From the parking you walk to the different beaches and calas.

Useful Tips

- Almost all the coves are crowded. Menorca is not like 20 years ago and tourists are everywhere in high season. - - - Don't expect empty beaches waiting for you.
- Get up early. From our experience, the coves start to get crowded by 10 am, and famous ones like Macarelleta, or Turqueta, even sooner. Try to get up early to avoid the masses and find parking.
- Bring your own food and drinks. There aren't so many beaches with facilities.
- Visit northern beaches. Probably you prefer the southern coastline – like us – but visiting the North is a must. Those red beaches transport you to a different planet.
- Bring your snorkel gear. The water is crystal clear and there are tons of fish! You won't regret.
- Be ready to walk. Some coves have their own parking, but that doesn't mean you'll be close to the water. In many cases, you'll need to walk 5-30 minutes to get to the beaches.

Best companies to rent a boat in Menorca
Generally, there are two main starting points for the boats: Ciutadella and Cala Galdana. I would suggest renting the boat in Ciutadella only if you're going to spend a full day on the boat. Otherwise, go to rent at Cala Galdana. Several companies offer 5-hour rentals and that's more than enough time to explore the southern coastline.

We strongly recommend IguanaBoats. Easy to reserve online, safe, simple, and nice boats. You won't need a license to rent them, and they'll give the basic information before you depart. It costs around 250-320 € depending on the season.

Where to rent a car in Menorca
After checking several websites like Europcar, Sixt and the other big companies... I saw in a blog a recommendation that was rated 10/10 and we absolutely recommend this company.

I'm talking about CochesMenorca. Cheaper than other multinational companies, they bring your car to the parking lot, a staff member guides you to the car and explains you everything in 10 minutes. No extra payments, no hidden info. 4.9/5.0 rate in Google. Nothing to add!

Historical Sites

Menorca is a hidden gem in the Mediterranean, boasting a rich history and cultural heritage that is just waiting to be explored. This small island is home to several historical sites that offer a captivating glimpse into its ancient past, making it a must-visit destination for anyone interested in history and archaeology.

One of the most well-preserved prehistoric monuments in Menorca is Naveta d'Es Tudons. This ancient megalithic chamber tomb dates back to the Bronze Age and is thought to have been used for the burial of the island's early inhabitants. Its unique shape and intricate stonework are a testament to the skill and craftsmanship of the island's prehistoric people.

La Mola Fortress is another historical site that should not be missed. Located in the port of Mahón, this 19th-century military complex offers stunning views of the surrounding area and is a testament to Menorca's strategic importance throughout history. Visitors can explore the fortifications, barracks, and watchtowers that were once used to defend the island from invaders.

Some other historical sites that you might want to consider exploring in Menorca include the Cathedral of Menorca, the Church of Santa Eulalia, and the Sant Antoni de Portmany Church. Each of these sites has its own unique history and architectural features that are sure to impress visitors.

Additionally, the Menorca Museum, located in the heart of Mahón, offers a comprehensive overview of the island's history, culture, and natural environment. The museum features a diverse collection of artifacts and exhibits, including displays on prehistoric Menorca, traditional crafts, and local flora and fauna.

Natural Wonders

Menorca being one of the four Balearic Islands is a paradise for nature lovers, outdoor enthusiasts, and anyone seeking a unique and unforgettable vacation experience. The island is known for its natural wonders, stunning beaches, crystal-clear waters, and unique geological formations, making it an ideal destination for those seeking to reconnect with nature and explore the beauty of the Mediterranean Sea.

One of Menorca's most captivating natural wonders is the Cova d'en Xoroi, a mesmerizing cave complex located on the island's southern coast. The cave is carved into the limestone rock and is famous for its breathtaking views of the Mediterranean Sea and its stunning rock formations. The cave complex is said to have been created by ancient geological processes millions of years ago, and it is a popular tourist attraction for those seeking a unique and memorable experience.

In addition to the Cova d'en Xoroi, Menorca is also home to numerous other natural wonders, including its pristine beaches and rugged coastline. Cala Macarella and Cala Mitjana are two of the most stunning beaches on the island, with their turquoise waters and white sandy shores providing the perfect backdrop for relaxation and leisure activities. The island's coastline is also dotted with numerous coves and bays, offering visitors a chance to explore the island's hidden gems and secret spots.

Menorca also boasts a unique geological formation known as the Algendar Gorge, a deep canyon carved into the limestone rock by the force of water over millions of years. The gorge is a popular hiking and trekking destination, offering stunning views of the surrounding landscape and a chance to connect with nature in a truly remarkable setting. The Algendar Gorge is a natural wonder that is not to be missed, and it's a testament to the power and beauty of nature.Menorca is a natural wonder in itself, with its diverse landscapes, stunning geological formations, and pristine beaches making it a paradise for nature lovers and outdoor enthusiasts alike. Whether it's exploring the Cova d'en Xoroi, relaxing on the beautiful beaches, or hiking through the Algendar Gorge, Menorca is a destination that is sure to leave a lasting impression on all who visit.

Popular Towns And Cities

Menorca a beautiful Spanish island boasts several charming towns and cities that attract tourists from all over the world. Each town has its own unique character, but they all offer a fantastic mix of history, culture, beautiful landscapes, and relaxing beach experiences.

One of the most popular towns to visit in Menorca is Mahón (Mao), the capital city of the island. Mahón is famous for its natural harbor, which is one of the largest in the world. The city offers a blend of history, culture, and stunning architecture. Visitors can explore the ancient walls of Fortaleza Isabel II, which was built in the 18th century to protect the city from pirates. They can also explore the historic city center, walk along the picturesque Port of Mahón, and immerse themselves in the local cuisine and vibrant nightlife.

Another beautiful town to visit in Menorca is Ciutadella, located on the western side of the island. Ciutadella is Menorca's ancient capital and is known for its elegant medieval architecture and historic charm. Visitors can wander through the narrow, winding streets of the old town, visit the impressive Cathedral of Ciutadella, and enjoy the beautiful harbor and vibrant squares. The city also hosts annual festivals, such as Sant Joan, which attracts thousands of visitors.

For those looking for a peaceful and tranquil atmosphere, Fornells is a small fishing village situated on the northern coast of Menorca. It is famous for its delicious seafood, especially the traditional lobster stew (caldereta de langosta). Visitors can stroll along the picturesque harbor, enjoy water sports like kayaking and sailing, or simply relax on the sandy beaches nearby.

Binibeca is another charming and picturesque fishing village located on the southern coast of Menorca. It showcases traditional whitewashed houses and narrow winding streets. Visitors can enjoy a leisurely walk through the village, visit the popular Binibeca Beach, and experience the laid-back atmosphere of Menorca's coastal life.

Alaior is a historic town situated in the center of Menorca, which boasts rich cultural heritage. The well-preserved old quarter features beautiful stone houses, narrow streets, and ancient gates. Visitors can explore the town's interesting architecture, visit the Church of Santa Eulalia, and enjoy the local cuisine in the traditional restaurants.

Es Mercadal is another charming rural village located in the center of Menorca. It is known for its authentic atmosphere and is an excellent starting point for hiking and biking adventures, with nearby routes leading to the highest point of the island, Monte Toro. The town also hosts the popular Festes de Sant Martí, a traditional festival featuring music, dancing, and delicious local food.

Finally, Santo Tomás is a popular beach resort situated on the southern coast of Menorca, which offers pristine sandy beaches and crystal-clear waters. It offers a peaceful and relaxed atmosphere, making it an ideal destination for those looking for a tranquil beach getaway. Visitors can enjoy sunbathing, swimming, and exploring the nearby coastal trails.

These towns and cities in Menorca offer a fantastic mix of history, culture, beautiful landscapes, and relaxing beach experiences.

Activities

Water Sports

Menorca is a true paradise for water sports enthusiasts. This small island is blessed with crystal-clear waters, diverse marine life, and an abundance of beaches and coves, providing a unique opportunity to experience the Mediterranean Sea in a new and exciting way.

One of the most popular water sports in Menorca is snorkeling, thanks to the island's rich underwater ecosystem and countless sheltered bays. Many of the island's beaches, such as Cala en Brut and Cala Galdana, are ideal for snorkeling, offering stunning underwater landscapes filled with colorful marine life, caves, and rock formations. The warm and calm waters of Menorca's bays make it an ideal location for beginners and experienced snorkelers.

If you are looking for a more adventurous experience, scuba diving is a major draw for water enthusiasts, with numerous diving centers across the island offering courses and guided dives for both beginners and experienced divers. Menorca's waters are home to a variety of dive sites, including underwater caves, shipwrecks, and vibrant coral reefs, providing an unforgettable diving experience.

For those who love wind-based sports, windsurfing and kiteboarding are popular activities due to the island's consistent wind conditions. Fornells, a fishing village on the island's north coast, is a particularly renowned spot for wind-based sports, offering equipment rental and lessons for all skill levels. The wind conditions are perfect for adrenaline junkies who are seeking a thrill.

If you prefer a more relaxed experience, kayaking and paddleboarding are other fantastic ways to explore Menorca's coastline, with rental companies located in many of the island's beach resorts. The calm and clear waters of the island make these activities enjoyable and accessible for all ages, offering the opportunity to visit hidden coves and secluded beaches along the rugged coastline.

In addition, sailing and boat trips are fantastic ways to experience the island from a different perspective. From leisurely cruises along the coast to exhilarating excursions to neighboring islands, there are plenty of options for those looking to take to the sea in a more relaxed manner. The island's coastline is dotted with charming fishing villages and secluded bays, providing a breathtaking backdrop for your sailing adventure.

Hiking And Nature Trails

With its diverse landscape, the island offers a range of hiking trails that make it an ideal destination for nature enthusiasts. From rocky cliffs and secluded coves to lush forests and wetlands, Menorca's trails offer a chance to explore the island's natural beauty and immerse oneself in its rich ecosystem.

One of the most notable hiking trails in Menorca is the Camí de Cavalls. This ancient path circumnavigates the entire island and offers a diverse range of landscapes, making it a popular choice for hikers of all levels. The trail is divided into multiple stages, with each segment offering unique terrain and scenery. Along the way, hikers can explore historical landmarks, charming fishing villages, and breathtaking coastal vistas.

Another popular hiking destination in Menorca is Monte Toro, the island's highest peak. A paved road leads to the peak, where a 17th-century sanctuary, a statue of the Virgin Mary, and a small café await visitors. The surrounding area provides opportunities for leisurely strolls and birdwatching, with the possibility of spotting native wildlife such as the Menorcan lizard.

The Albufera des Grau Natural Park is another protected natural area in Menorca that offers well-marked trails through wetlands, marshes, and diverse bird species. The park provides a tranquil setting for nature walks and is a birdwatching haven, with the bird observatory being the perfect spot to observe herons, ducks, and other waterfowl.

For those looking for a unique hiking experience, the Barranc d'Algendar is a must-visit destination. This ravine is known for its unique geological formations and rich biodiversity. Hiking through the gorge, visitors can admire ancient rock formations, limestone cliffs, and verdant vegetation. The trail offers a fascinating look at the island's geological history and provides an excellent opportunity for nature photography.

It's essential to note that proper footwear, water, and sun protection are essential for a safe and enjoyable hiking experience. Additionally, hikers should be mindful of their surroundings and follow the Leave No Trace principles to minimize their impact on the environment.

Cultural Events

Menorca is an island that is rich in history and culture. The island has a diverse array of cultural events and celebrations that take place throughout the year and reflect the unique traditions of the island. From ancient festivals rooted in paganism to modern artistic showcases, visitors to Menorca can immerse themselves in a wide range of cultural experiences.

One of the most important and widely observed events in Menorca is the Sant Joan Festival, which is celebrated annually on June 23rd and 24th. The festival is deeply rooted in tradition and features a series of rituals, including the famous "Jaleo," a vibrant horse parade where riders make their steeds rear up on their hind legs amidst a lively crowd. The festival also includes musical performances, sports competitions, traditional dancing, and fireworks displays. Various towns and villages across the island participate in the festivities, with Ciutadella's celebrations being the largest and most renowned.

Another cultural festival that takes place in Menorca is Tardor a Menorca or Autumn in Menorca. This event features a wide range of activities, including art exhibitions, live music performances, theater productions, and culinary events showcasing Menorcan cuisine. Visitors have the opportunity to engage with local artists, artisans, and musicians and can also attend workshops and seminars to learn about the island's traditional crafts and customs. Tardor a Menorca takes place from September to November.

The International Music Festival of Summer is also a popular event that takes place during the months of July and August. This festival highlights a diverse range of musical genres, including classical, jazz, and world music. Renowned musicians, orchestras, and ensembles from around the world come to Menorca to perform in various historical venues, such as churches, courtyards, and theaters. The festival creates a vibrant atmosphere, attracting music enthusiasts and fostering cultural exchange through the universal language of music.

If you happen to be on the island in September, Festes de Gràcia is an annual celebration that takes place in the charming town of Mahón during the first week of September. Festes de Gràcia features a lively program of events, including parades, traditional dances, street markets, and concerts. One of the highlights is the ceremonial "Jewels of Menorca" parade, where locals dress in traditional attire and showcase the island's cultural heritage through colorful and vibrant performances.

Menorca Horse Fiestas are another exciting spectacle that takes place on the island from June to September each year. The fiestas consist of religious ceremonies, live entertainment, food, and parades. Local horses are raced through the streets, and riders show off their skills with Jaleos, where horses stand and jump on their hind legs while the brave in the crowd try to 'touch the heart' of the horse, as it is believed to bring good luck. If you want to sample some real Menorcan culture, we recommend going along to one of the many Horse Fiestas taking place during the summer months.

In addition to these major events, Menorca hosts numerous smaller festivals, religious pilgrimages, and cultural gatherings throughout the year, each with its unique traditions and customs. Whether it's celebrating the island's patron saints, participating in local craft fairs, or enjoying traditional music and dance, visitors to Menorca are sure to find an enriching cultural experience that offers insight into the island's heritage and vibrant community.

Nightlife

While the island is not as famous for its nightlife as some other Mediterranean destinations, it still offers a variety of options for evening entertainment. From lively beach bars to vibrant nightclubs and atmospheric live music venues, the nightlife in Menorca offers a diverse range of experiences to suit different tastes and preferences.

The island's main towns, Ciutadella and Mahón, are the epicenters of Menorca's nightlife scene. These charming towns offer a mix of atmospheric bars, pubs, and clubs that cater to different tastes and preferences. One of the distinct features of Menorca's nightlife is the emphasis on relaxed and social gatherings, which often take place in outdoor settings or picturesque locations.

If you're looking for a laid-back evening experience, the harborfront bars in Ciutadella and Mahón are perfect. These establishments offer a laid-back ambiance, perfect for enjoying cocktails or local wines while taking in stunning views of the marina and the surrounding architecture. From here, visitors can also take a stroll along the waterfront and soak up the lively atmosphere.

Beach bars are another popular option for those seeking a more relaxed nightlife experience. Menorca's beautiful coastline is dotted with beach bars that come alive in the evenings. Visitors can unwind with a drink while listening to the sound of the waves and watching the sunset. Some beach bars also host occasional live music performances, creating a relaxing and intimate atmosphere.

For those looking for a more energetic nightlife experience, there are several clubs and late-night venues in Ciutadella and Mahón. While Menorca may not be known for its mega clubs, the island still offers a vibrant club scene. Visitors can find clubs and late-night bars that cater to those looking for dancing and electronic music. Whether you're a seasoned clubber or just looking for a fun night out, Menorca's nightlife scene has something for everyone.

One of the popular nightclubs in Menorca is Sa Terrassa, located in Ciutadella. This open-air club offers a stunning rooftop terrace with panoramic views and a vibrant atmosphere. It hosts regular DJ sets and themed parties, making it a popular spot for those seeking a lively evening. The club's unique setting and stunning views make it a must-visit destination for those looking for a memorable night out.

Another iconic club in Menorca is Cova d'en Xoroi, perched on the cliffs of Cala en Porter. This music bar and club is carved into the natural caves, offering breathtaking views of the Mediterranean. Known for its unique setting and diverse music offerings, Cova d'en Xoroi is an unforgettable nightlife destination.

It's important to note that the nightlife in Menorca has a more relaxed and laid-back vibe compared to other party destinations, and venues typically close earlier. However, this doesn't diminish the enjoyment of the nightlife experience, as it provides an opportunity to unwind and socialize in beautiful surroundings.

In addition to the bars and clubs, Menorca also offers a variety of live music venues. From intimate jazz clubs to large concert halls, the island's music scene is diverse and exciting. Many bars and restaurants also host live music performances, providing a relaxed and enjoyable atmosphere for visitors to enjoy.

Best Things To Do After Dinner

One of the best things to do after dinner in Menorca is to head to Pont d'en Gil, located on the western side of the island, a short 10-minute drive from the town of Ciutadella de Menorca. This remarkable section of the Menorcan coastline is a cool spot for sunsets, and the view is simply spectacular when the light dips low and the sun glows red and pink across the Balearic Sea. You can even see the outline of the Majorcan mountains in the distance when it's clear. There's a mirador lookout point that gazes directly at the iconic rock arch of Pont d'en Gil itself, making it a perfect spot for couples or those on a budget.

If you're looking for a buzzing strip that fizzes with life from morning until night, head to Moll de Llevant in Mahon, the island's capital. It's easy to reach by foot from virtually anywhere in the town, while yachters can moor up right on the side in one of the dedicated harbors. Come a summer's evening, this place is usually pumping with people. There are hearty Balearic cerveza beer stops like El Alquimista, next to sleek mixology cocktail lounges like Sa Falua. And you get the poker tables and rotating blackjack wheels of the Casino Maritim.

For those looking for some fine dining and drinks, head to Moll de Ponent, which is a wide, palm-sprouting boulevard that threads through the center of Mahon town, linking the main ferry port with a whole string of tempting tapas lounges and bars. After dark, the south side of the Moll de Ponent is typically a cacophony of clinking wine glasses and sizzling plates of Catalan and Menorcan foods. You'll also find fine places to watch the cruise ships coming and going at night, such as the Mirador Costa des General lookout, along with intriguing modern art galleries like ATICA.

Another place that nightlife seekers on the island of Menorca simply cannot ignore is the Puerto Antiguo de Ciutadella de Menorca, a deep harbor that cuts into the main town on the western side of the island, bursting into life when the sun dips. You'll find the main bar cluster on the south side of Puerto Antiguo, there, look for the likes of ever-energetic Es Cau, a favorite with the spritz-drinking crowd. Or there's Dreams & Drinks, a courtyard cocktail lounge shaded by umbrellas. Throw in a handful of tasty tapas kitchen, and you've got a fully made night on the town.

Finally, for a romantic evening stroll, head to Passeig des Moll, which promises to slow down the pace of an evening and get those romantic vibes flowing. It runs along the northern side of the Puerto Antiguo de Ciutadella de Menorca, the main port area in the town of Ciutadella. You can reach it on foot from the town center in about 5 minutes. In the place of happening tapas kitchens and sidewalk bars, you'll find a cobbled promenade in the shadow of a 15th-century medieval fortification. Beyond that, boats of all shapes and sizes bob at the moorings in the harbor. After dark, there are some gorgeous photo ops to be had, courtesy of the brightly lit buildings that spill down to the water on the opposite side.

Dining

Local Cuisine

The traditional cuisine of Menorca features a wide variety of fresh seafood, locally grown fruits and vegetables, and a range of delicious dairy products. One of the most popular and distinctive dishes of Menorcan cuisine is Caldereta de Langosta, a flavorful lobster stew that is often prepared with the island's famous Mahón cheese. The dish is made with fresh lobster, potatoes, tomatoes, and onions, with a touch of garlic, olive oil, paprika, and saffron. The Mahón cheese is added towards the end of the cooking process, giving the stew a rich and creamy texture.

The island's close proximity to the sea also means that a wide variety of seafood dishes are enjoyed here, including grilled fish, seafood paella, and caldereta de pescado (fish stew). The seafood is always fresh and cooked to perfection, and the flavors are enhanced by the use of local herbs, spices, and olive oil.

Menorca is also known for its delicious and unique cheeses, with Mahón cheese being the most famous. This aged cow's milk cheese has a strong and tangy flavor and is often enjoyed with local bread, olives, and honey. Other popular cheeses on the island include formatge de Mao and formatjades. Another traditional dairy product of Menorca is the rich and creamy flao, a dessert made with cheese, eggs, and mint.

In addition to seafood and dairy products, Menorcan cuisine also features a variety of meat dishes, such as sobrassada, a spreadable cured sausage made with pork, paprika, and other spices. Other popular meat dishes include carn i xua, a type of cured, spiced pork, and grilled lamb. The meat is always of the highest quality and is often cooked over an open flame, giving it a delicious smoky flavor.

The island's fertile soil and mild climate also make it ideal for growing a wide variety of fruits and vegetables, which are heavily featured in Menorcan cuisine. The local dishes are often accompanied by fresh salads, roasted vegetables, and a variety of seasonal fruits. Menorcan tomatoes, peppers, and aubergines are particularly famous for their sweet and intense flavors.

When it comes to beverages, Menorca is known for its locally produced gin, which is often enjoyed in cocktails such as the popular Pomada, made with gin and lemonade. The gin is made with juniper berries, which grow wild on the island, giving it a unique and distinctive flavor. Additionally, the island's terrace bars and cafes are a great place to enjoy a glass of local wine or a refreshing glass of pomada.

Here is a closer look at ten of the island's most popular dishes and food items.

1. Caldereta de Langosta - A delicious and hearty lobster stew that is a traditional Menorcan dish. Made with fresh local seafood, potatoes, and flavored with the island's famous Mahón cheese, this stew is a mouth-watering treat that is perfect for a chilly evening. The dish is often served with crusty bread or rice, and it pairs perfectly with a glass of Menorcan wine.

2. Arroz de la Mar - A classic seafood paella that is a staple of Menorcan cuisine. Made with local rice, fresh seafood, and fragrant herbs and spices, this dish is bursting with flavor and is perfect for sharing with family and friends. The dish is often cooked in a large, shallow pan, which allows the rice to cook evenly and absorb all the flavors of the seafood and spices.

3. Mahón Cheese - A popular and unique cheese made from cow's milk, known for its tangy and robust flavor. This cheese is a must-try for cheese lovers and is perfect for pairing with local wines or enjoying on its own. The cheese is often served with bread, olives, and other local meats.

4. Sobrassada - A spreadable cured sausage made with pork, paprika, and other local spices, often enjoyed with bread or in various dishes. This flavorful sausage is a staple of Menorcan cuisine and is perfect for adding a little kick to any meal. The sausage is often used as a topping for pizza or in sandwiches.

5. Carn i Xua - A type of cured, spiced pork that is a staple in Menorcan cuisine, usually served sliced and accompanied by local bread. This flavorful meat is perfect for a quick snack or as part of a larger meal. The meat is often marinated in garlic, paprika, and other spices to give it a unique and delicious flavor.

6. Gambas a la Menorquina - Shrimp prepared in a traditional Menorcan style, often cooked with garlic, tomatoes, and olive oil. This dish is a must-try for seafood lovers and is perfect for those who enjoy bold, Mediterranean flavors. The shrimp is often served with rice or bread, and it pairs perfectly with a glass of Menorcan wine.

7. Ensaïmada - A sweet pastry made with flour, water, sugar, eggs, and lard, often served as a dessert or with coffee. This delicious pastry is a staple of Menorcan cuisine and is perfect for satisfying a sweet tooth. The pastry is often served plain or with powdered sugar, but it can also be filled with chocolate, cream, or other sweet fillings.

8. Caldereta de Cordero - A rich and flavorful lamb stew, cooked with a variety of local herbs and vegetables. This hearty dish is perfect for a chilly evening and is sure to warm you up from the inside out. The stew is often served with crusty bread or rice, and it pairs perfectly with a glass of Menorcan wine.

9. Flao - A traditional Menorcan dessert made with cheese, eggs, and mint, giving it a unique and refreshing flavor. This delicious dessert is perfect for those who enjoy lighter, more refreshing desserts and is perfect for enjoying after a meal. The dessert is often served cold, and it pairs perfectly with a cup of coffee or tea.

10. Menorcan Wine - Locally produced wines, including reds, whites, and rosés, made from the island's vineyards and enjoyed throughout the region. These delicious wines are perfect for pairing with local cuisine or enjoying on their own and are a must-try for wine lovers. The wines are often made using local grape varieties, and they are known for their unique and delicious flavors.

Popular Restaurants

Here are some of the best restaurants in Menorca that you should definitely check out:

1. Restaurant S'Amarador - Located in Carrer de Pere Capllonch, 42, Ciutadella de Menorca, Balearic Islands, Spain, this Michelin-guide restaurant specialises in locally caught and traditionally cooked seafood. The menu includes dishes like fritter calamari and marinara paella, but the standout dish is the sprawling lobster platter that's served with fries and fried eggs. Opening hours are from Monday to Sunday from 1 pm to 4 pm and from 8 pm to 11 pm, except Wednesdays when it's closed.

2. Taps Can Avelino - This restaurant is located in Carrer Sínia des Muret, 39, Maó, Balearic Islands, Spain and is one of the standout Menorcan kitchens in the capital city. The menu offers hearty south Spanish staples mingling surf and turf with a zest of North African spice. Standout dishes include breaded shrimp in mango sauce, pepper-crusted Mojama tuna steaks, and Iberian ham cuts with taboulé salad. Opening hours are from Tuesday to Sunday from 1 pm to 4 pm and from 7 pm to 11.30 pm, closed on Mondays.

3. Can Xavi - Located in S'Arraval, 1, Mahón, Balearic Islands, Spain, this restaurant spills out of the medieval buildings in the very heart of Mahon's town centre, offering sun-kissed seating areas where S'Arraval street meets Plaça Bastió. The tapas-sharing plates are usually the go-to at Can Xavi, including bruschetta with Balearic tomatoes, meatballs in tomato passata, and stacks of salty French fries to match. Opening hours are from Monday to Saturday from 10 am to 4.30 pm and from 7 pm to 11.30 pm, closed on Sundays.

4. Restaurante España - This restaurant is located in Carrer Victori, 48, Es Castell, Balearic Islands, Spain and serves traditional Spanish food and all the local favourites. Classic Spanish dishes include paella, spicy prawns, patatas bravas, and gazpacho soups. The setting is charming but not overly fancy, with a big bar space and a small al fresco area in the back terrace. Opening hours are from Thursday to Saturday from 1 pm to 4 pm and from 7 pm to 11 pm, Sunday to Wednesday from 1 pm to 4 pm and from 7.30 pm to 11.30 pm.

5. Pinzell - This restaurant offers a rather modern take on the age-old cooking of Spain and the Balearics. The restaurant sits on the Plaça dels Pins, just a short walk from the marinas of Ciutadella de Menorca. The menu is all about fresh, locally available ingredients cooked honestly and with flair. Expect grilled octopus with roast potatoes and watercress, sirloin steaks served with thick-cut chips, and paprika-rich stews with langoustines and fish broth. Opening hours are from Monday to Sunday from 12 pm to 4 pm and from 7 pm to 11 pm.

6. Sa Lliga - This restaurant is located in Camí des Castell, 10, Mahón, Balearic Islands, Spain and is known for its creative and innovative cuisine. The menu features dishes like prawn carpaccio, roasted lamb, and homemade desserts. The restaurant also offers an extensive wine list that pairs well with the dishes. Opening hours are from Monday to Saturday from 1 pm to 3.30 pm and from 8 pm to 11 pm, closed on Sundays.

7. Es Tast de na Silvia - This restaurant is located in Carrer d'Artrutx, 20, Ciutadella de Menorca, Balearic Islands, Spain and is run by chef Silvia Anglada. The menu features traditional Menorcan cuisine with a contemporary twist. Some of the dishes include Menorcan cheese ravioli, roasted suckling pig, and almond ice cream. The restaurant also offers a tasting menu that changes regularly. Opening hours are from Tuesday to Saturday from 1 pm to 3.30 pm and from 8 pm to 10.30 pm, closed on Sundays and Mondays.

8. Ses Forquilles - This restaurant is located in Carrer de Sant Cristòfol, 3, Mahón, Balearic Islands, Spain and offers a fusion of Mediterranean and Asian cuisine. The menu features dishes like tuna tataki, sushi, and tempura prawns. The restaurant also offers a vegetarian and gluten-free menu. Opening hours are from Monday to Saturday from 1 pm to 3.30 pm and from 8 pm to 11 pm, closed on Sundays.

9. Es Tast de Mar - This restaurant is located in Carrer de Sant Joan, 6, Fornells, Balearic Islands, Spain and offers stunning sea views. The menu features dishes like lobster stew, grilled octopus, and rice with squid ink. The restaurant also offers a tasting menu and a children's menu. Opening hours are from Monday to Sunday from 1 pm to 4 pm and from 7.30 pm to 10.30 pm.

10. Es Moli de Foc - This restaurant is located in Carrer de Sant Esteve, 2, Ferreries, Balearic Islands, Spain and is housed in a restored flour mill. The menu features dishes like grilled meats, roasted fish, and homemade desserts. The restaurant also offers an extensive wine list. Opening hours are from Tuesday to Saturday from 1 pm to 3.30 pm and from 7.30 pm to 10.30 pm, closed on Sundays and Mondays.

Shopping

1. Mercat des Peix: Located in the heart of Menorca's capital, Mahon, Mercat des Peix is a historic and bustling fish market that has been around since the mid-1920s. The market is known for offering the best selection of fresh fish and seafood on the island. It features traditional vendors and street food stalls and is partly covered. The lively atmosphere draws locals and tourists alike. Apart from fish and seafood, the market also offers a variety of local Menorcan products like cheeses, meats, and sweets. There are also numerous tapas and wine bars around the alleys, making it a perfect place to relax and enjoy a snack and drink between purchases.

2. Mercat Municipal: Mercat Municipal is the main market in the historic town of Ciutadella and occupies a gorgeous late-1800s building with large archways around its exterior. It is the perfect place to enjoy a blend of traditional and modern Menorcan cuisine. The market is packed with local vendors selling fresh seafood, charcuterie, cheeses, and wines. There are a few tapas bars to sit back at the end of the day and enjoy a chat with locals. The market is open most days of the week with a separate morning and afternoon shift, closing for a siesta after lunch. While a lively place at any time, Mercat Municipal is particularly busy on Saturday mornings.

3. Mercat de Sant Francesc: Located in the heart of Mahon, Mercat de Sant Francesc is a popular outdoor market that offers a wide variety of fresh produce, meats, cheeses, and local Menorcan products. The market is particularly known for its olive oil, which is considered one of the best in the world. Apart from food, the market also has a wide variety of stalls selling clothing, handmade crafts, and souvenirs. It is a perfect place to explore the local culture and enjoy the vibrant atmosphere.

4. Plaça dels Pins: Plaça dels Pins is a lively square located in the center of Ciutadella that transforms into a bustling market every Friday. The market offers a wide variety of products, including traditional Menorcan handicrafts, souvenirs, clothing, and local produce. The square is surrounded by numerous cafes and restaurants, making it a perfect place to relax and enjoy a snack or a drink. The market is particularly popular among tourists and locals alike.

5. Plaça de la Catedral: Plaça de la Catedral is located in the heart of the historic town of Ciutadella and is one of the main tourist attractions on the island. The cobble-stone streets surrounding the cathedral are home to a variety of shops and restaurants. From clothing to footwear, it's an excellent place to shop for local fashion. You can also find cafes with sidewalk seating, which are great for relaxing and people-watching in the afternoon.

6. Placa del Mercat: Placa del Mercat is a lively square in the center of Mahon that transforms into a bustling market every Tuesday and Saturday. The market offers a wide variety of products, including fresh produce, meats, cheese, and local Menorcan products. The square is surrounded by numerous cafes and restaurants, making it a perfect place to relax and enjoy a snack or a drink. The market is particularly popular among locals.

7. Fornells Market: Fornells Market is a popular market located in the picturesque village of Fornells, known for its fresh seafood. The market offers a wide variety of local Menorcan produce, including fruits, vegetables, meats, and cheese. You can also find numerous stalls selling handmade crafts, clothing, and souvenirs. The market is particularly popular among tourists.

8. Es Mercadal Market: Es Mercadal Market is a traditional market located in the center of the village of Es Mercadal. The market offers a wide variety of local Menorcan produce, including fruits, vegetables, meats, and cheese. You can also find numerous stalls selling handmade crafts, clothing, and souvenirs. The market is particularly popular among locals.

9. Sant Lluis Market: Sant Lluis Market is a traditional market located in the center of the village of Sant Lluis. The market offers a wide variety of local Menorcan produce, including fruits, vegetables, meats, and cheese. You can also find numerous stalls selling handmade crafts, clothing, and souvenirs. The market is particularly popular among locals.

10. Ciutadella Night Market: Ciutadella Night Market is a lively market that takes place every summer evening in the center of Ciutadella. The market offers a wide variety of products, including traditional Menorcan handicrafts, souvenirs, clothing, and local produce. The market is particularly popular among tourists and locals alike and is a perfect place to enjoy the vibrant atmosphere of the town.

Unique Local Products

Menorca is a haven for those seeking unique, locally made products that reflect the island's rich heritage and culture. From traditional handicrafts to culinary delights, visitors have a wide range of distinctive items to choose from. Here are some of the standout local products that you must check out during your trip to Menorca:

1. Mahón Cheese: This famous cheese is named after the island's capital, Mahón. It is made from cow's milk and aged for a specific period, resulting in a distinctive flavor and texture. The cheese comes in different varieties, ranging from buttery and mild to sharp and tangy. Mahón cheese is a perfect edible souvenir that captures the essence of Menorcan gastronomy.

2. Avarques: Avarques are traditional Menorcan leather sandals with a distinctive design. Handcrafted by local artisans, these sandals are known for their durable yet comfortable construction. Avarques are available in a variety of colors and styles, making them a popular and unique footwear option for visitors to the island.

3. Gin Xoriguer: Menorca has a strong gin-making tradition, and one of the iconic products is Gin Xoriguer. This gin has been produced on the island for centuries and is made using traditional distillation methods. It has a unique flavor profile and is often enjoyed in the form of a pomada, a refreshing cocktail made with gin and lemonade.

4. Pottery: Menorca is renowned for its distinctive pottery, which is characterized by its rustic charm and earthy hues. Skilled potters create an array of products ranging from tableware and decorative items to traditional cooking vessels. Each piece of Menorcan pottery tells a story of the island's heritage and craftsmanship.

5. Menorcan Wines: The island has a burgeoning wine industry, with vineyards producing a variety of excellent wines. Visitors can sample and purchase local wines that showcase the unique terroir of Menorca. Some wineries offer guided tours and tastings, providing an opportunity to savor the flavors of the island.

6. Embroidery and Lacework: Menorca has a long-standing tradition of intricate embroidery and lacework. Local artisans skillfully create delicate and beautiful pieces, including table linens, clothing embellishments, and decorative textiles. These handcrafted items are a testament to the island's artistic legacy and make for an exquisite souvenir.

Overall, Menorca's locally made products are an essential part of the island's cultural heritage, and they offer a unique opportunity to take a piece of the island home with you. So, make sure to explore the local markets and shops during your trip to Menorca and discover the best of what the island has to offer.

Practical Tips

This stunning destination boasts a pleasant climate throughout the year, making it an ideal vacation spot for travelers seeking a warm and sunny getaway.

The best time to visit Menorca is during the spring and summer months, from April to September. During this time, you can enjoy the island's stunning beaches and outdoor activities, such as hiking, biking, and water sports, in the most comfortable climate.

In the spring (April to June), temperatures are mild, ranging from 16-24°C (61-75°F). This is the ideal time to explore the island's lush landscapes, hike along the Camí de Cavalls coastal path, and visit the charming towns and villages without the summer crowds. You'll also get to witness the blossoming of wildflowers and the awakening of the island's flora and fauna, making it a perfect time for nature lovers.

Summer (July to September) is the peak tourist season in Menorca, with temperatures reaching 28-32°C (82-90°F). This is the perfect time for beach lovers to enjoy the crystal-clear waters and soak up the sun on the island's numerous sandy beaches. It's also a great time to participate in water sports such as snorkeling, diving, and sailing. You can also attend various cultural events and festivals during this time, such as the Sant Joan Festival, which is one of the island's biggest celebrations.

In the fall (October), the weather starts to cool down, with temperatures ranging from 17-24°C (63-75°F). The island is less crowded during this time, making it a great opportunity to explore Menorca's historical and cultural sites, including its UNESCO-listed prehistoric Talayotic monuments. You can also take nature walks and experience the beautiful autumn foliage.

Winter (November to March) is the off-peak season, with temperatures ranging from 9-15°C (48-59°F). While the weather may be cooler and occasional rain showers are possible, it's still a good time to visit if you're interested in hiking, birdwatching, and exploring the island's natural beauty without the crowds. You can also visit local markets and shops to get a taste of the island's traditional cuisine and products.

Overall, the best time to visit Menorca is from April to September when the weather is warm and sunny, and the island is buzzing with life and activities. Whether you prefer lounging on the beach, exploring historical sites, or enjoying outdoor adventures, Menorca has something to offer for every traveler.

Local Customs And Etiquettes

It's important to understand and respect these traditions to make the most of your experience. Here are some of the local customs and etiquettes of Menorca in detail:

1. Siesta: Siesta, the midday rest, is still widely observed in Menorca. Many shops and businesses close for a few hours in the afternoon to rest and recharge. It's important to be aware of this custom and plan your activities around the siesta time, typically between 2 p.m. and 5 p.m. During this time, you can relax, enjoy a leisurely lunch or take a stroll around the island.

2. Respect for mealtimes: Menorcans consider lunch to be the main meal of the day and often enjoy it with family and friends. It is customary to take your time and savor the meal. Dinner is generally eaten later in the evening, typically after 8 p.m. It's considered polite to respect these mealtime traditions when dining out in Menorca. You can enjoy local delicacies such as seafood, paella, and ensaimadas while experiencing the island's culture.

3. Greetings: When meeting someone in Menorca, it's customary to greet them with a handshake and maintain strong eye contact. Spanish greetings such as "buenos días" (good morning), "buenas tardes" (good afternoon), and "buenas noches" (good evening) are commonly used and appreciated. Menorcans are hospitable people who will appreciate your efforts to learn a few basic phrases in their language.

4. Clothing: Menorcans typically dress stylishly and modestly, especially when visiting churches, religious sites, or formal events. It's important to dress respectfully when visiting religious sites or attending cultural events. You can wear comfortable and light clothes while exploring the island during the day, but it's better to dress up a bit for formal events.

5. Public behavior: Public displays of affection are common in Spain, including Menorca, but it's important to be mindful of the level of affection shown in certain settings, especially in more traditional or conservative areas. Menorcans are friendly and welcoming people who respect each other's privacy and personal space.

6. Language: While Spanish is the official language, the Menorcan dialect (Catalan) is also widely spoken. Learning a few basic phrases in Catalan, such as "bon dia" (good morning) or "gràcies" (thank you), can be greatly appreciated by the locals. You can also use English as it's widely spoken on the island.

7. Tipping: Tipping is not obligatory in Spain, but it is a common practice to leave a small tip at restaurants and for other services, especially if you've received excellent service. A tip of around 5-10% is generally appreciated. You can also show your appreciation by leaving positive reviews or recommending the services to others.

By understanding and observing these local customs and etiquettes, you can show your respect for Menorcan culture and gain a deeper appreciation for the island's traditions and way of life.

Health And Safety

When visiting Menorca as a tourist, it is essential to consider health and safety to ensure a pleasant and trouble-free experience. Here are some specific aspects to keep in mind:

1. Medical Facilities: Menorca has modern medical facilities, including public and private hospitals, clinics, and pharmacies. Care is generally of a high standard, and European Union visitors with a European Health Insurance Card (EHIC) can access necessary healthcare. However, it is advisable for all travelers to have comprehensive travel insurance to cover any medical expenses. It's also essential to remember to bring any necessary prescription medication with you, along with a copy of your prescription to avoid any misunderstandings or issues.

2. Food and Water Safety: The tap water in Menorca is generally safe to drink, but some visitors may prefer to drink bottled water. Food hygiene standards are typically good in restaurants and cafes, but it's always wise to use caution with street food and ensure that meat and seafood are cooked thoroughly to prevent any related health issues. It's also worth noting that Menorca has a vibrant food culture, with plenty of local delicacies to try, so make sure to savor the flavors while staying safe.

3. Sun Safety: Menorca enjoys a sunny Mediterranean climate. It is crucial for tourists to protect themselves from the sun's strong rays by using sunscreen, wearing hats, and seeking shade, particularly during peak sun hours. Sunburn and heat-related illnesses can be avoided by practicing proper sun safety measures. It's also worth noting that the sun can be particularly strong in Menorca, so it's important to be extra vigilant about sun protection.

4. Beach and Water Safety: Menorca's beautiful beaches are a major attraction. While enjoying water activities, it's important to be mindful of any warning signs related to strong currents or rough seas. Adhering to any safety guidelines and being aware of the flag system used on beaches to indicate water safety for swimming is important. It's also essential to remember that the sea can be unpredictable, so it's best to take precautions and stay safe.

5. Driving and Transportation: If planning to drive in Menorca, it is essential to understand local traffic regulations and road conditions. Visitors must adhere to speed limits and drive cautiously on narrow roads, especially in rural areas. Public transportation, such as buses and taxis, generally offer safe and reliable options for getting around the island. If renting a car, it's worth familiarizing yourself with the local driving laws and regulations.

6. Personal Safety: Menorca is known for its safety and low crime rates. However, it is wise to exercise general caution and be conscious of personal belongings, especially in crowded tourist areas. It's also worth noting that Menorca has a relaxed and welcoming atmosphere, so tourists should feel comfortable exploring the island and getting to know the locals.

7. Weather Considerations: Menorca experiences a Mediterranean climate, which means hot, dry summers and mild, wet winters. Visitors should be prepared for the weather conditions expected during their stay and take necessary measures to stay safe and comfortable. It's also worth noting that the weather can be changeable, so it's best to be prepared for any eventuality.

Useful Phrases And Vocabularies

Remember, Menorca is a part of Catalonia, so you'll notice some Catalan influence in the language. These phrases should help you navigate common situations on the island.

Greetings:
- Hello: Hola
- Good morning: Bon día
- Good afternoon: Bona tarda
- Good evening/night: Bona nit

Common Expressions:
- Please: Si us plau
- Thank you: Gràcies
- Excuse me: Perdoni
- Yes: Sí
- No: No
- Sorry: Ho sento

Basic Questions:
- What is your name?: Com et dius?
- How are you?: Com estàs?
- Where is...?: On és...?

Directions:
- Left: Esquerra
- Right: Dreta
- Straight ahead: Tot recte
- Where is the beach?: On és la platja?

Eating Out:
- Menu: Carta
- Water: Aigua
- Food: Menjar
- I would like...: Voldria...
- The bill, please: El compte, si us plau

Numbers:
- 1: Un
- 2: Dos
- 3: Tres
- 4: Quatre
- 5: Cinc

Time:
- Now: Ara
- Today: Avui
- Tomorrow: Demà
- Yesterday: Ahir
- What time is it?: Quina hora és?

Emergencies:
- Help!: Ajuda!
- Emergency: Emergència
- I need a doctor: Necessito un metge
- Police: Policia

At the Airport:
- Can you help me find my luggage?: Em podeu ajudar a trobar el meu equipatge?
- Where is the departure gate?: On és la porta de sortida?

Accommodation:
- I have a reservation: Tinc una reserva
- Is breakfast included?: L'esmorzar està inclòs?
- The room is too hot/cold: L'habitació fa massa calor/fred

Shopping:
- How much does this cost?: Quant val això?
- Do you accept credit cards?: Accepteu targetes de crèdit?
- I'm just browsing: Només estic mirant

Transportation:
- Where is the bus station?: On és l'estació d'autobusos?
- How much is a taxi to the city center?: Quant costa un taxi al centre de la ciutat?
- Is there a train to...?: Hi ha un tren cap a...?

Activities:
- What is there to do around here?: Què hi ha per fer per aquí?
- Can you recommend a good restaurant?: Podeu recomanar-me un bon restaurant?
- I'd like to book a tour: Voldria reservar una excursió

Weather:
- What's the weather like today?: Com és el temps avui?
- It's raining: Està plovent
- It's sunny: Fa sol

Health:
- I don't feel well: No em trobo bé
- Where is the nearest pharmacy?: On és la farmàcia més propera?
- I have allergies: Tinc al·lèrgies

Local Cuisine:
- I'd like to try a local dish: Voldria provar un plat típic
- What do you recommend from the menu?: Què recomaneu del menú?
- Is this dish spicy?: Aquest plat és picant?

Beach and Leisure:
- Can you recommend a nice beach?: Podeu recomanar una platja bonica?
- Are there water sports activities available?: Hi ha activitats d'esports aquàtics disponibles?
- I need sunscreen: Necessito protector solar

Cultural Interactions:
- Tell me about local customs: Expliqueu-me sobre les costums locals
- Is there a traditional festival happening soon?: Hi ha un festival tradicional properament?
- I'd like to learn more about your culture: Voldria aprendre més sobre la vostra cultura

Tourist Information:
- Where is the tourist information center?: On és el centre d'informació turística?
- Can you provide a map of the city?: Podeu proporcionar-me un mapa de la ciutat?
- Are there guided tours available?: Hi ha visites guiades disponibles?

Public Transportation:
- How often do buses/trains run?: Amb quina freqüència passen els autobusos/trens?
- Is there a day pass for public transportation?: Hi ha un abonament de transport públic diari?
- Which bus/train goes to the historical center?: Quin autobús/tren va al centre històric?

Navigating Streets:
- Can you point me to the nearest landmark?: Em podeu indicar cap al punt de referència més proper?
- I'm lost. Can you help me find my way back to the hotel?: Estic perdut. Em podeu ajudar a tornar a l'hotel?
- Is this street pedestrian-friendly?: Aquest carrer és apte per als vianants?

Dining Etiquette:
- Is tipping customary in restaurants?: És habitual deixar propina als restaurants?
- Are there vegetarian/vegan options on the menu?: Hi ha opcions vegetarianes/veganes al menú?
- What time do restaurants usually close?: A quina hora tanquen normalment els restaurants?

Emergency Services:
- Where is the nearest hospital?: On és l'hospital més proper?
- How do I contact emergency services?: Com puc contactar amb els serveis d'emergència?
- I've lost my passport. What should I do?: He perdut el meu passaport. Què hauria de fer?

Shopping Assistance:
- Is there a duty-free shop at the airport?: Hi ha una botiga lliure de taxes a l'aeroport?
- Can I get a refund for this item if I change my mind?: Puc obtenir un reemborsament per aquest article si canvio d'opinió?
- Where is the nearest shopping district?: On és el districte de compres més proper?

WiFi and Connectivity:
- Is there free WiFi available in public places?: Hi ha WiFi gratuït disponible als llocs públics?
- Can you recommend a good internet cafe?: Podeu recomanar-me un bon cibercafé?
- How do I connect to the local network?: Com puc connectar-me a la xarxa local?

Entertainment Options:

- Are there any live music performances tonight?: Hi ha alguna actuació de música en directe aquesta nit?
- What are the popular nightlife spots in the city?: Quins són els llocs de vida nocturna més populars a la ciutat?
- Can you recommend a good place to watch the sunset?: Podeu recomanar-me un bon lloc per veure la posta de sol?

These phrases should make it easier for tourists to navigate Menorca and have a more enjoyable experience.

Positive Affirmations

Positive affirmations are a powerful tool that can help you improve your mental and physical well-being. These are short, positive statements that you can repeat to yourself every day, either in the morning or at night before going to bed. By doing so, you can train your brain to focus on the positive aspects of your life and shift your mindset towards a more optimistic outlook.

Studies suggest that affirmations can be a simple yet effective way to reduce symptoms of anxiety and depression, and boost overall self-esteem. Repeating positive phrases can help you develop a more positive self-image, and help you appreciate your strengths and abilities. Additionally, affirmations can help strengthen the neural pathways in the brain, leading to better mental function and cognitive performance.

But the benefits of affirmations are not limited to mental health. They can also have a positive impact on your physical health. For instance, studies have found that repeating affirmations can lower stress levels, which can improve cardiovascular health and reduce the risk of chronic diseases.

Positive affirmations can be easily incorporated into your daily routine, and they can be used by people of all ages. Whether you're looking to reduce stress, boost self-esteem, or improve your overall health, positive affirmations are a great place to start. By practicing affirmations, you can create a more positive and optimistic outlook on life, which can have a profound effect on your well-being. So, if you want to improve your mental and physical health, why not give positive affirmations a try today?

- You can do it . You're unstoppable
- and inspiring.
- I am having a positive and inspiring impact on the people I come into contact with.
- I am inspiring people through my work.
- I'm rising above the thoughts that are trying to make me angry or afraid.
- Today is a phenomenal day.
- I am turning DOWN the volume of negativity in my life, while simultaneously turning UP the volume of positivity.
- I am filled with focus.
- I am not pushed by my problems; I am led by my dreams.
- I am grateful for everything I have in my life.
- I am independent and self-sufficient.
- I can be whatever I want to be.
- I am not defined my by past; I am driven by my future.
- I use obstacles to motivate me to learn and grow.
- Today will be a productive day.
- I am intelligent and focused.
- I feel more grateful each day.
- I am getting healthier every day.
- Each and every day, I am getting closer to achieving my goals.
- Through the power of my thoughts and words, incredible transformations are happening in me and within my life right now.
- I am constantly growing and evolving into a better person.
- I'm freeing myself from all destructive doubt and fear.

- My soul radiates from the inside and warms the souls of others.
- I don't compare myself to others. The only person I compare myself to is the person I was yesterday. And as long as the person I am today is even the tiniest bit better than the person I was yesterday —I'm meeting my own definition of success.
- Note to self: I am going to make you so proud.
- I finish what matters and let go of what does not.
- I feed my spirit. I train my body. I focus my mind. This is my time.
- My life has meaning. What I do has meaning. My actions are meaningful and inspiring.
- What I have done today was the best I was able to do today. And for that, I am thankful.
- One small positive thought in the morning can change my whole day. So, today I rise with a powerful thought to set the tone and allow success to reverberate through every moment of my day.
- I set goals and go after them with all the determination I can muster. When I do this, my own skills and talents will take me to places that amaze me.
- Happiness is a choice, and today I choose to be happy.
- I am worthy of what I desire.
- I choose myself.

- I am resilient in the face of challenges.
- I am proud of myself and my achievements.
- I will accomplish everything I need to do today.
- I do my best, and my best is good enough.
- I prioritize my well-being.
- I overcome my fears by getting out of my comfort zone.
- I am love, and I am loved.
- Money comes frequently and easily to me.
- I trust my inner guidance and follow it.
- I accept my emotions and let them move through me.
- I take care of myself, mind, body, and spirit.
- I trust myself to make the right decisions.
- I give myself permission to take up space.
- I use my voice to speak up for myself and others.
- I trust that I'm heading in the right direction.
- I allow myself to make mistakes as they help me grow.
- I accept myself exactly as I am without judgment.
- I have everything I need to achieve my goals.
- I am constantly generating brilliant ideas.
- I am safe and supported.
- I love and accept myself.
- I am kind to myself and others.

- I accept myself for who I am and create peace, power and confidence of mind and of heart.
- I am going to forgive myself and free myself. I deserve to forgive and be forgiven.
- I am healing and strengthening every day.
- I've made it through hard times before, and I've come out stronger and better because of them. I'm going to make it through this.
- I do not waste away a single day of my life. I squeeze every ounce of value out of each of my days on this planet—today, tomorrow, and everyday.
- I must remember the incredible power I possess within me to achieve anything I desire.
- I do not engage with people who try to penetrate my mind with unhelpful thoughts and ideas—I walk away when a person or a situation isn't healthy for me.
- I belong in this world; there are people that care about me and my worth.
- My past might be ugly, but I am still beautiful.
- I have made mistakes, but I will not let them define me.

Essential Informations

Menorca Airport, also known as Mahon Airport (MAH), is a small but efficient airport located on the southeast coast of the island, just under 3 miles (4.5 km) from Mahón - the capital city of Menorca. The airport is the sole airport on the island and is served by all major budget European and British airlines, making it easy to find flights and plan your arrival.

Transportation options to and from the airport are quite good. If you prefer to take a taxi, you can easily find one at the rank outside the airport. The fares for each destination are transparently displayed on a pillar in the arrivals hall, with prices starting at €15 for journeys in the southeast and rising up to €70 for resorts in the west. However, note that Uber does not operate in Menorca.

Alternatively, you can take the public bus, which is the cheapest option. There's only one bus to/from the airport, which takes you to/from Mahon's bus station in about 15 minutes (€2.75 per person). The service is frequent, and from the bus station, you can connect to a bus to most towns and holiday resort hubs on the island.

If you plan to explore the island on your own, renting a car is a great option. The airport is the cheapest place to pick up a hire car in Menorca. If you're looking for prices and availability, the best place to start looking for the island is Rentalcars.com as it lists most local companies as well as the major rental brands.

Within the airport, the Caixabank ATM charges a fee if you wish to withdraw money, so it's always a good idea to have some cash on hand. There's also a helpful tourism office if you need advice, help, or maps.

For those who are interested in the local culture, it's worth noting that locals speak Menorcan (Menorquí), a dialect of Catalan, and they will also speak Castillian, which is usually known or referred to as 'standard' Spanish. Many signs will display only the Catalan or include both languages, and it's also why several places have two names: Mao / Mahón, Binibequer / Binibeca, Isla del Rey / Illa Del Rei. On bus signs and schedules, the Catalan name takes precedence.

If you plan to visit Menorca, it's important to know the best time to visit. The unofficial tourism season begins on May 1st and runs through to the end of September or mid-October. During this time, all businesses are open, and coastal transport connections are increased. The average temperatures during this time are May (13-21°C), June (17-25°C), and July (20-28°C+). However, the crowds can be overwhelming during the high season, which is from mid-July to the end of August/beginning of September. Accommodation costs will be quite high during this time, and early starts and afternoon breaks or respite in the shade will be essential.

The late summer 'shoulder season', from mid-September to the end of October, is a great time to visit. The crowds are more manageable, prices are on a downward trend, all businesses and services are still in full operation, and the Mediterranean sea is deliciously warm. The cooler temperatures also make hiking much more enjoyable. The only con to bear in mind is that the chances of changeable or overcast weather increase as the season progresses, so it's always a good idea to pack appropriately.

You might be wondering how long you should stay to experience all that this beautiful island has to offer. Well, based on our experience, we would say that a week is perfect for a holiday and first-time visit to experience the highlights, whilst 10-14 days would only be ideal if you are happy to travel slow and adore either walking or the beaches.

Menorca has a sedate pace and layout, which can make a two-week stay a bit too long of a stretch for some visitors. However, if you do opt for a longer stay, we would highly recommend switching your base after a week so that you can focus on getting to know different parts of the island intimately and minimize repetitive driving stretches. This way, you will be able to experience the island's diversity and charm to its fullest.

On the other hand, if you're looking for a shorter visit, Menorca has plenty to offer even for a long weekend or 4-day spontaneous break in the early or later summer. The size and connections of Mahón and Ciutadella make them good options for a shorter trip.

However, it's worth mentioning that on shorter trips, it's unlikely that you'll visit both of these cities. Mahón is located in the east, whilst the old capital of Ciutadella is in the west, so pairing them both in a week-long visit may not be desirable or practical depending on where you're based. Instead, you may want to focus on exploring the beaches, hiking trails, and other natural wonders of Menorca.

When planning a trip to Menorca, there are a few things that one must keep in mind. For instance, if you're looking to save some money, it's recommended that you do your 'big shop' outside of the two main cities, namely Mahón and Ciutadella. The supermarkets located on the outskirts of these cities are significantly cheaper than the small supermarkets found in tourist hubs. This means that you could save up to 50% on many items. Nonetheless, we would encourage you to support local businesses as much as possible, and the small supermarkets in tourist areas are still ideal for stocking up your kitchen or sourcing snacks and drinks for your day trip.

It's also important to note that wind plays a vital role on the island, and everything, from beach plans to boat trips, depends on the direction and speed of the wind. Locals make their plans according to the wind's direction, and if you're visiting Menorca, it's wise to follow suit. If the northern Tramontane wind is blowing, it's best to head to the southern beaches and towns, and if the south wind is blowing, go to the northern beaches and towns. Checking the forecast and winds is essential if you're planning on renting a boat or going on a boat trip.

Moreover, Menorca follows a siesta culture, and many shops, businesses, restaurants, and cafes close around 2 pm, only to reopen around 4-5 pm. Therefore, it's a good idea to adjust your body clock if you're visiting for a week or longer. Eating later in Menorca, say around 8-9 pm, is also the best way to avoid being the only people in an empty but popular restaurant.

When it comes to eating out, reservations are essential, especially during the peak summer season. In fact, we'd recommend reserving almost everywhere, sometimes up to a couple of days in advance, especially if you're planning to eat out on the weekends. While Menorca has some excellent restaurants, they can be quite pricey, so it's best to keep that in mind while planning your budget. However, there are a few exceptions, such as the fish market in Mahón and some of the lower quality tourist-centric resort restaurants.

11 Facts About Menorca

1. Menorca is not only famous for its beaches and beautiful views, but it is also the birthplace of mayonnaise. The story goes that during the 18th century occupation by the French, the famous eggy condiment was taken back to Paris where it was presented at a victory banquet. The rest, as they say, is history. The name of the sauce also comes from the island's capital, Mahon, hence Salsa Mahonesa.

2. The Cami de Cavalls or The Path of Horses is a unique attraction of Menorca. This 185-mile track cuts around the edge of the island and was originally used as a defensive network against invasion dating back to the 14th century. Its 20 stages are unsurprisingly extremely popular with hikers, and you can navigate part or the whole path on horseback (taking around a week).

3. Menorca's rich maritime history is partly down to its constant invasion and occupation by foreign forces, thanks largely to the island's strategic position and huge natural harbour. After Pearl Harbor in Hawaii, Menorca's capital city Mahon claims the largest natural harbour in the world. It's still very much active and a buzzing hub of island life.

4. Gin culture has taken root and flourished on the island, thanks to the British invaders. Menorca's most famous brand and popular export, Xoriguer, is the go-to gin and the most popular drink is the Pomada – a simple and refreshing mix of gin and cloudy lemonade served ice-cold.

5. Menorca was declared a Unesco Biosphere Reserve in 1993 due to its amazing diversity of flora and fauna, and landscape that ranges from beaches and valleys, to caves, wetlands, and sand dunes. Beyond a few pockets of development blighting the coastline, the island is a beautiful expanse of natural beauty, much concentrated in the eastern S'Albufera des Grau Natural Park, which is home to numerous bird and amphibian species.

6. Boasting an impressive 1,500 megalithic sites, Menorca is a veritable paradise for archaeologists, history buffs, or anyone interested in ancient civilizations. The wealth of archaeological remains provides a fascinating insight into the architectural and cultural heritage of the island's earliest inhabitants, and there are key sites to visit all over the island, including villages, burial tombs, and an incredible necropolis in a system of caves carved out of the rocks.

7. While Menorquins retain a fiercely independent sense of their own identity, the island is still very much part of Spain, and the mostly easterly of its Iberian outposts. Therefore, it's the first piece of Spanish soil to see the sun each morning, and with uninterrupted views across the Mediterranean, home to some of the most spectacular sunrises.

8. Menorca's distinctive orange-rind Mahón cheese is a must-try when visiting the island. It has earned a much-coveted Denominación de Origen classification and comes in three main types: young and mild, semi-cured, and the potently-flavored fully cured. Hardened cheese-lovers, however, should try the mature añejo variety – they're over a year old and have a spicy kick akin to Parmesan.

9. The tallest hill and highest point on the island, Monte Toro, is considered the spiritual center of Menorca and has been a place of pilgrimage since the 13th century. Not only can you visit the Sanctuary that was built by the Augustin monks in the 17th century, step outside and you can take in incredible panoramic sea views across the whole length of the island.

10. Menorca has more beach than Mallorca and Ibiza combined. With around 220 kilometers (137 miles) of coastline and around 180 kilometers (112 miles) of that being beach. While much of it is inaccessible by car, there are still scores of beaches within easy reach, and with a combination of pretty little coves and sweeping sandy bays, it includes some of the finest beaches in the world.

11. Menorca has strong historical and cultural Catalonian roots, just like its bigger brother Mallorca. The most obvious manifestation of this is in their language, Menorquín, which is considered by most a Catalan dialect (though some claim it deserves to be labeled a language in its own right). All inhabitants are also fluent in Castilian – or mainland Spanish – with plenty also proficient in the likes of English and German. Menorcans are proud of their heritage and often showcase their traditions and customs in festivals throughout the year.

Conclusion

Menorca is a stunning island gem that is not only incredibly beautiful, but also rich in history, culture, and natural wonders. From its turquoise waters and white sandy beaches to its charming villages and delicious local cuisine, Menorca offers something for everyone. Whether you are looking for a peaceful getaway, an adventure-filled holiday, or a cultural experience, Menorca has it all.

The travel guide to Menorca provides a comprehensive overview of all the island has to offer, making it the perfect companion to any trip. From the best places to visit and things to do, to the most delicious foods to try and the most convenient ways to get around, the guide offers all the information you need to have a successful and enjoyable trip.

One of the most appealing things about Menorca is its natural beauty. The island is home to some of the most breathtaking landscapes in the Mediterranean, with stunning beaches, crystal-clear waters, and lush greenery. Whether you want to relax on the beach, swim in the sea, or explore the island's natural wonders, Menorca has plenty to offer.

But Menorca is not just about its natural beauty. The island is also rich in history and culture, with a fascinating past that can be seen in its ancient monuments, museums, and cultural events. From the prehistoric Talayotic ruins to the charming old towns and historic landmarks, Menorca is a destination that will captivate even the most discerning travelers.

And let's not forget about the food. Menorca has a rich culinary tradition that is based on fresh, local ingredients and traditional recipes. From the famous Mahón cheese and the tasty sobrasada sausage, to the delicious seafood and the refreshing local gin, Menorca's cuisine is a true delight for the taste buds.

Whether you are traveling solo, with friends or family, Menorca is a destination that will leave you with unforgettable memories. It is a place where you can escape the hustle and bustle of daily life and immerse yourself in a world of natural beauty, culture, and relaxation. So, pack your bags, grab your travel guide, and get ready to discover the magic of Menorca.

Copyrighted Material

Printed in Great Britain
by Amazon

41207978R00046